GET SMART ABOUT
ELON MUSK

Adam Kent

Get Smart about Elon Musk
by Adam Kent

Published by Rocket Books, Inc.
New York, NY, USA

Copyright © 2023 Rocket Books, Inc.

Disclaimer: Please note the information contained within this document is for educational and entertainment purposes only. All effort has been executed to present accurate, up to date, and reliable, complete information. No warranties of any kind are declared or implied. The content within this book has been derived from different sources. By reading this document the reader agrees that under no circumstances is the author responsible for any losses, direct or indirect, which are incurred as a result of the use of information contained within the document, including, but not limited to, - errors, commissions, or inaccuracies.

For kids...
who dream big,
who work hard to become better,
who get up when they fall,
who know we are all human and
all worthy of respect and success.

For my son Little Adam...
who lights up my life.

May your dreams come true.

This book is for you.

ABOUT THIS BOOK

This biography book is meant to be a fun, brief and inspirational look at the life of a famous person. Reading biographies can help learn from people who have experienced extraordinary things. While you read through the books in this series, think about how their experiences can help you in your own life!

As you read this book you will find bolded words. There are definitions of the words at the end of each page. You will also find interesting facts at the end of each chapter. Plus, there are some questions to get you thinking at the end of the book.

I hope you enjoy learning about this extraordinary person!

Have a great time reading,

Adam Kent

CONTENTS

GET SMART ABOUT
ELON MUSK

Adam Kent

ELON MUSK
AT A GLANCE

Elon Musk is a South African-born American entrepreneur who is also famously known to be the richest man in the world as of 2022. He is a big dreamer known for founding several important companies such as Tesla Motors and SpaceX that have aimed to really change the world.

ELON MUSK
FAST FACTS

1. Elon Musk actually invented a video game at the young age of 12 that he sold at the same age.

2. Elon was born in South Africa to a mother who was a successful model and a father who was an entrepreneur.

3. Elon was accepted into the prestigious Stanford University to study for an advanced degree program to get a PhD after college, but he then dropped out shortly after.

4. Elon is the founder of an early electric car company and a space exploration company. His goal is to change the world.

5. As of 2022, Elon Musk has eight known children. He believes it is important for the survival of humans on Earth to have more children.

CHAPTER 1
THE EARLY DAYS

Elon Musk was born in Pretoria, South Africa, on June 28, 1971. As a young child, Elon was known for being a big dreamer. In fact, he spent so much time lost in thought about invention ideas and daydreaming that his parents and doctors became worried that he may have a hearing problem! Eventually, they even decided to have his hearing checked. Doctors thought his problem could be related to his tonsils, so he ended up having his tonsils removed! Can you believe it? Elon's dreaming continued though.

Elon and his siblings, a brother and sister, were raised by both parents in the same home as little kids. Their parents ended up getting a divorce, though, when Elon was just ten years old. The siblings then spent most of their youth in a single parent household.

Initially, Elon and his siblings chose to stay with his mother, who was a Canadian model. Life with his mother was not always easy. Money was limited. In fact, Elon's mother even had to work five jobs at one point just to make enough money to support the Elon and his siblings.

A couple of years after his parents divorced, though, Elon chose to leave his mother's care and live mainly with his father. His father was a wealthy, traveling entrepreneur.

Elon's decision to live with his father changed his lifestyle dramatically compared to how he lived with his mother at the time. After moving to live with his father, Elon was then exposed to a **lavish** lifestyle that was filled with vacations, yachts, which are fancy sailboats, skiing and expensive computers. Money suddenly was no longer a problem.

---

lavish /'la-vish/ adjective 1: a large amount <example: a lavish display flowers> 2: given in large amounts <example: he received lavish praise> verb: to give in large amounts <example: he lavished her with praise>

His relationship with his father was mixed. There were things about his father that Elon struggled with. He didn't like many of the things his father did.

The exciting adventures he had and his father's **diverse** business **ventures** likely helped form who Elon Musk is today in terms of his businesses and helped prepare him for some of his exciting successes.

---

diverse /dī-'vərs/ adjective 1: different or unlike *<example: diverse interests>* 2: made up of things or people that are different *<example: diverse groups of people>*

venture /'ven(t)-shər / noun 1: an act that involves risk *<example: business venture>* verb 1: to guess at the risk of being wrong or criticised *<example: venture a guess>* 2: to go even though there is risk *<example: venture into the forest>*

In grade school, Elon was known by classmates to be small, quiet and an **avid** reader. In his late childhood, he developed a big interest in computers. He was so interested in computers that he even taught himself how to program!

In recent years, coding and computer programming has become more well-known and popular with many kids, but back when Elon was young, this was not the case. Believe it or not, when he was just 12 years old, Elon Musk sold his first computer game! It

---

avid /ˈa-vəd/ adjective: having great enthusiasm or excitement for something *<example: an avid football fan>*

was a game he created that he called "Blaster." This was a unique accomplishment for a boy his age, especially during the time he was growing up.

Elon Musk doesn't remember his elementary school and high school years fondly. They were hard. Elon was a bookworm and didn't make many friends.

More importantly, Elon was bullied a lot during school. The bullying started when he was young and continued until he was 15 years old.

At 15 years old, Elon entered into a growth spurt and became bigger. At that time, he had a change of attitude. He decided to defend himself against the bullies. He took up karate lessons to learn the best ways to do that. He also took up wrestling. All the hard work paid off and Elon started to defend himself successfully.

Elon Musk stayed in South Africa until he was 17. He graduated from high school early. Then, he moved to Canada where his mother and sister were. He went there to head to college.

CHAPTER 1
FUN FACTS

1. Pretoria, the city where Elon Musk was born, is one of three capital cities in South Africa. Yes, that's three! Normally, states or countries have just one capital. South Africa is indeed unique with three: Pretoria, Cape Town and Bloemfontein.

2. Elon Musk had his tonsils removed as a child. Tonsils are in the back of the mouth. They help our bodies remove bacteria and viruses. However, they become easily infected. When people get frequent infections in their tonsils, sometimes their doctors

recommend that they have them removed.

3. Elon Musk trained in karate to help fight against bullying as a teenager. "Karate" comes from two words in Japanese, "kara" which means "empty" and "te" which means "hand."

4. Elon Musk actually started computer programming as a young child. The world's first known computer programmer in the world was a woman! Her name is Ada Lovelace. She programmed a mechanical (one that is non-electrical) computer. This was a long time ago, in 1842.

5. Elon Musk made a video game called Blastar that he sold when he was just 12 years old. The first video game ever is often thought to be called Pong, which was made in 1971. However, it is more likely a game called Tennis for Two, invented by a physicist named William Higinbotham.

CHAPTER 2
FAMILY MATTERS

Elon Musk was born to parents named Maye and Errol Musk. Maye Musk played a significant role in shaping Elon Musk's early life and upbringing. Her support and encouragement are often cited as key factors in his journey as an entrepreneur and innovator.

Maye is a Canadian-American model, registered **dietitian-**nutritionist, and speaker. She was born on April 19, 1948, in Canada. Her modeling career began in the 1960s, and she has since become known for embracing her natural silver hair and challenging beauty standards by breaking age-related norms.

Aside from her modeling career, Maye Musk also has two master's degrees in dietetics and nutritional sciences. She used her education not just for her work as a professional dietician for decades, but also to ensure her family made healthy choices and got proper nutrition.

---

dietician /dī-ə-ˈti-shən/ noun: a specialist that uses the science of nutrition to plan diets or food that people eat *<example: A dietician helped me lose weight.>*

As a mother, Maye Musk's diverse achievements and her ability to defy stereotypes continue to inspire individuals across generations to embrace their passions and pursue success in their chosen fields. Errol Musk, Elon's father is a South African electromechanical **engineer** and pilot. He was born on May 3, 1946, in South Africa. Errol Musk's influence on Elon's career as an entrepreneur and innovator has undoubtedly played a role in

---

engineer /ˌen-jə-ˈnir/ noun: a person who designs and builds useful machines (such as computers) or structures (such as buildings or roads) *<example: an electrical engineer>* verb: to plan, build or manage as a professional engineer *<example: He engineered a plan to improve the safety of the railroad track.>*

shaping his journey.

Errol Musk's professional pursuits have primarily centered around engineering and technology. He was involved in projects related to mining and sustainable energy solutions. He also has a private pilot's license. His interest in aviation led him to pursue piloting as a hobby. His father was self-employed and a successful **entrepreneur**. His adventurous spirit surely impacted Elon's thirst for exploration himself.

---

entrepreneur /ˌän-trə-p(r)ə-'nər/ noun: a person who tries to make money by starting a business and managing it, as a company or alone, and all the risks that go with it <example: She wanted to become an entrepreneur and start her own real estate business.>

Elon Musk has a younger brother named Kimbal. Kimbal Musk was born on September 20, 1972.

Kimbal Musk is an entrepreneur like Elon. He and Elon worked together over the past few decades. Together they co-founded Zip2 Corporation, an online business directory in the 1990s. This venture marked his entry into the world of technology and entrepreneurship.

In recent years, Kimbal has shifted his focus to the food industry and sustainable farming. He opened a line of restaurants that serve locally sourced and organic ingredients. He also started the "Big Green" initiative, which helps create learning gardens in schools, teaching children about healthy food choices.

While Elon Musk is widely recognized for his contributions to technology and space exploration, Kimbal Musk has carved his own path to promote environmentally friendly changes in the world.

Tosca Musk is Elon Musk's younger sister. She was born on July 20, 1974, in South Africa. The family lived together there until 1981, when Kimbal and Elon went to live with their father, Errol, and Tosca stayed with their mother, Maye. After high school, Maye and Tosca moved to Canada. Elon followed and moved there within the following year.

Tosca has made her mark in the entertainment industry as a producer and director of films. Tosca Musk also is the founder of Passionflix, which is a streaming service that creates movies from romance books.

Beyond her work in the entertainment industry, Tosca Musk also works to promote equal opportunities for women and is also known for her advocacy for gender equality and women's representation in media. Her efforts extend to creating opportunities for female filmmakers and storytellers to share their voices and perspectives.

CHAPTER 2
FUN FACTS

1. In the 1980's Elon Musk's father Errol was on his way from South Africa to England to sell a small plane he owned. On the way their flight was interrupted, and they accidentally met Italian businessmen who wanted to buy the plane and gave him part ownership of an emerald mine as payment. That is the story of how he became a part owner of an emerald mine. Errol Musk took emeralds from the mine and then sold them to jewellers around the world as he travelled and made a lot of money.

2. Emeralds are a valuable green gemstone. They are also the birthstone of the month of May.

CHAPTER 3
A UNIQUE EDUCATION

After his high school years, Elon moved to Canada. He attended Queen's University while there. He moved primarily because he had wanted to avoid having to serve in the military in South Africa.

Because it is easier to become a Canadian **citizen** first, he decided

---

citizen /ˈsi-tə-zən/ noun 1: a person who lives in a certain place 2: a person who legally belongs to a certain place and has the rights and protections of that place *<example: a citizen of Canada>*

to move to Canada first. Elon's mother is originally from Canada, so, it was an easy decision to move there. He did first become a Canadian citizen as he had planned. Later he later became a U.S. citizen in 2002.

In 1992, Elon attended the University of Pennsylvania. He first studied **economics** and after **physics**. He received two bachelor's degrees from the school. Later, he was accepted to the famous Stanford University in California

---

economics /ˌe-kə-'nä-miks/ noun: the study of how wealth is created by the making and selling of goods and services *<example: He studied economics in school.>*

physics /'fi-ziks/ noun: a science that deals with matter and energy and the interactions of both <*example: the study of physics.*

into a PhD program for physics. Stanford is known as one of the top universities in the world, so this was a big accomplishment.

In a daring move, just two days after he started the PhD program, Elon decided to drop out of the school! Elon decided he wanted to start a business instead of going to school. He wanted to start his first company. He wanted to become an entrepreneur. Do you think that was a smart move? Let's find out!

CHAPTER 3
FUN FACTS

1. Canada is the world's second largest country. On a map, it is right above, just north of, the United States of America.

2. Stanford University is a famous university in California near San Francisco. It ranks as one of the best universities in the world.

3. Mandatory military service is called conscription. This means that when men or men and women turn a certain age, (such as 18 years old) they must serve in the military. Conscription is not common in the world. Most

countries do not require military service. Of the countries that do, only some require all people of a certain age to serve.

4. South Africa stopped mandatory military service in 1994, but this was after Elon Musk decided to move to Canada for university.

CHAPTER 4
A CAREER TO REMEMBER

In 1995, after leaving his PhD program at Stanford University in California in a bold move after just two days, Elon Musk launched his first company. He called the new business the "Zip2 Corporation." He started the company with his brother Kimbal.

Zip2

Zip2 was a tech company that developed an online city guide. The city guide was a list of places in cities that people living in or visiting the city could visit.

The idea of Zip2 was to license the city guide to other companies. These companies could use the guide for their business purposes. The company was a great success that gained big name **clients** such as *The New York Times* and the *Chicago Tribune*. Zip2 was such a success that it was sold just four years after it was started, in 1999. Can you guess how much it was

---

client /ˈklī-ənt/ noun: a person who uses the service of another *<example: a lawyer's clients>*

sold for? You might find this hard to believe, but it was sold for over a whopping $300 million!

X.com

Elon and Kimbal Musk used the money from their sale of Zip2 to start a new business venture. They called this second business "X.com." X.com was an online payments company. Just a year into the business, X.com purchased another company and combined the two companies into one. That newly formed company led to what is known today as PayPal. Have you heard of PayPal? Many people use Paypal to pay for things online.

Just 3 years after starting X.com, which later became Paypal, the company was sold. Can you guess how much it was sold for? The company was sold for a value of $1.5 billion! That is a lot of money!

You may have heard of the company that bought it: eBay. Elon owned only a small portion of the company, at 11%, but it was a huge success.

SpaceX

Can you guess what Elon did with the money he made from X.com? If you guessed that he started *another* business, you are right!

In 2002, Elon Musk founded his third company which he called Space Exploration Technologies Corporation, or "SpaceX" for short. SpaceX was created with the vision of building spacecraft to use for eventual **commercial** space travel. That is exciting!

After many unfortunate trials and tribulations, SpaceX was finally awarded a major contract from NASA. This was quite a major feat for the famous company. Shortly after, SpaceX sent a rocket called "Falcon 9" to space! Elon was so

---

commercial /kə-ˈmər-shəl/ noun: an advertisement on internet, radio or television *<example: a television commercial>* adjective: related to the buying and selling of goods and services *<example: a commercial real estate property>*

excited about it. At the time, he described the event saying, "I feel very lucky. ... For us, it's like winning the Super Bowl."

SpaceX's first major launch of cargo was in 2012. On May 22 of International Space Station with over 1,000 pounds of supplies for the astronauts there.

Over the next several years, after going through more trials and **tribulations**, SpaceX completed more awesome accomplishments. For instance, in 2013, SpaceX launched a **satellite** that followed

---

satellite /ˈsa-tə-ˌlīt/ noun: something that orbits or exists near to another of larger size *<example: a satellite in space>*

tribulation /ˌtri-byə-'lā-shən/ noun: a hard or distressing experience *<example: the tribulations of a difficult relationship>*

the path of the Earth's rotation. In 2015, they launched another Falcon 9 rocket. The plan was designed to allow the rocket to carry a satellite called the "Deep Space Climate Observatory (or DSCOVR)." The satellite was created so scientists could observe how the sun's energy impacts power grids and communication systems on Earth.

In addition, in 2018, SpaceX launched another Falcon rocket called "Falcon Heavy," which was equipped with some extra rocket boosters in order to help it take extra heavy machinery even farther into space than before.

The goal was to use such a rocket for deep space missions in the future. This launch was notable also because they added a cherry-red Tesla Roadster car with a spaceman dressed **mannequin** and cameras to take photos of the car's intended orbit around the sun. That is a first!

In 2017, Elon Musk set his eyes on the planet Mars. He presented a plan that year to design a rocket that could carry over 100 people and could make its way all the way to Mars. He set a goal of 2022 as the year SpaceX would launch the first cargo mission to Mars, with the goal of eventually bringing people there to live one day. This was a big goal! What do you

---

mannequin /ˈma-ni-kən/ noun: a form that represents a human figure used for various purposes but especially for hanging clothes

<example: She dressed the mannequin with her clothing designs.>

think about that? He called the rocket "BFR," which stood for "Big Falcon Rocket."

In late March 2018, SpaceX began to launch many satellites into space with the permission of the U.S. government. The goal of launching the satellites was to provide internet service around the world, especially in rural areas. The project is called "Starlink."

Starlink has been quite a **controversial** project. Many people believe it is good to help people in rural areas and make internet access easier. On the other hand, these satellites fill up and light up the sky. This may potentially cause

controversial /ˌkän-trə-ˈvər-shəl/ adjective: related to or causing disagreement or argument *<example: a controversial decision>* problems to arise in the future for astronomers studying space.

Tesla

Do you remember that the company SpaceX was started in 2002 with the money that Elon had made from the sale of his other company X.com? Well, Elon started using the same money for another company as well. Are you surprised by that? I would bet that you're probably not!

This is the strategy that Elon seems to have followed much of his adult life with his businesses. The other new company was a car company. Can you guess the name of that car company? Well, the new car company was called "Tesla Motors." The goal of Tesla Motors was to make electric cars, batteries and solar roofs **affordable** and easily accessible to the public.

Actually, Elon Musk did not create Tesla Motors. Tesla Motors was originally created in 2003 by two men named Martin Eberhard and Marc Tarpenning. Elon Musk liked the company so much that he gave $6.5 million dollars to the company and became an owner of it. Elon was put in charge of developing the cars and other products for the company.

Since 2003, there have been a number or award-winning cars that

affordable /ə-ˈfȯr-də-bəl/ adjective: reasonably priced *<example: an affordable apartment>*

have been developed starting with the Tesla Roadster in 2008. These cars are **noteworthy** because they go very fast and are also electric, so they do not use gas, like most cars on the road today. Every time you charge a Tesla car, you can drive over 250 miles with it! The models of Tesla cars that people can currently buy as of 2022 include:

- Model S,
- Model 3,
- Model X
- Model Y

noteworthy /ˈnōt-ˌwər-thē/ adjective: worthy of attracting attention <*example: a noteworthy event*>

The original Tesla Roadster stopped production, but a second version of the Tesla Roadster is set to be released in the year 2023. Tesla Motors will also be releasing a mini truck called Cyber Truck and a Semi-truck, as well, but these are not expected to be released until 2023 at the earliest.

SolarCity and the Boring Company

You may have noticed that Elon Musk's companies so far have all had a goal of really changing the world. Elon helped create even more companies that had big goals of changing the world.

The next company is called "SolarCity Corporation." SolarCity was created in 2006 by Elon's cousin's Peter and Lyndon Rive with Elon's help. SolarCity is a solar energy company that focuses on helping home and business owners across America start using solar panels for energy. In 2016, Tesla Motors and SolarCity combined.

Another company is called "The Boring Company." Elon Musk started The Boring Company in 2017. What do you think of that name?! You may think that it is funny to give such a dull word to a big company with big dreams. It is true! However, did you know that bore has another meaning? Bore also means to make a hole.

The Boring Company bores holes in the ground to make tunnels! These tunnels are going to be used to reduce traffic in major cities around the United States. Now you see the name is quite clever! One thing for sure is with all these interesting world changing companies Elon has created and worked with, Elon Musk is certainly not boring!

Twitter

In 2022, Elon Musk surprised the world by offering to buy Twitter. This was a big shock and at first it was not clear if he was serious. He was! In October, he officially bought Twitter and became the CEO.

Over the first year heading Twitter, Elon made many changes. He fired a lot of people to save on costs and also started charging a monthly fee for certain ways to use Twitter, while it remained free for others.

Many of Elon Musk's choices with Twitter sparked public debate. Many people liked his choices, and many people didn't. Elon responded by asking in a poll he posted to Twitter if he should step down as CEO and hire someone else in his place. He said he would do what the public voted him to do. The public voted that he should step down; so, he did! In June of 2023 Elon Musk was replaced as CEO by Linda Yuccarino. In July of 2023, Elon Musk changed the name of Twitter to X. This also sparked much debate.

The future will tell what becomes of X and what new accomplishments Elon Musk Will achieve in his incredible career. Maybe the best way to explain Elon Musk's overall career goals is to use his own words. In 2017, Elon Musk tweeted: "My goals are to accelerate the world's **transition** to sustainable energy and to help make humanity a multi-planet civilization, a consequence of which will be the creation of hundreds of thousands of jobs and a more inspiring future for all.

transition /tran(t)-ˈsi-shən/ noun: a change or shift from one to another state, subject or place *<example: transition of power>*

ADAM KENT

CHAPTER 4
FUN FACTS

1. NASA was opened in 1958 in the United States. The goal of NASA was space exploration. One of the first goals of NASA was to have a man walk on the moon. NASA reached this goal, and the first man walked on the moon, in 1969.

2. Tesla Motors was named after the scientist and inventor Nikola Tesla, who was born in 1856. Nikola Tesla held over 300 patents for his inventions. He is thought to be the inventor of alternating current (AC) which was used in many types of

common products such as radios, telephones, and toys. Nikola Tesla is also thought to be the first on record person to suggest the idea of solar energy.

3. Mars is sometimes called the Red Planet, but it is not hot. It is very, very cold. Mars is the fourth planet from the sun. It is 142 million miles from the sun. It also orbits around the sun, like Earth. It is smaller than Earth.

4. Solar power is the world's most abundant and cheapest source of energy. It is also currently the fastest growing energy source in the world as of 2022.

CHAPTER 5
HOBBIES AND PASSIONS

In addition to the many money-making businesses that he has created and been involved with, throughout his life, Elon Musk has also started one called a non-profit organization. A "non-profit" is an organization developed to help give back to the world without focusing on trying to make money back like businesses do. You can think of non-profits like charities.

The name of Elon Musk's non-profit is the "Musk Foundation." Money that is given to the Musk Foundation is used for things that Elon Musk has been interested in and focused on with his businesses.

For example, the Musk Foundation gives money toward space exploration activities and toward activities intended to help the world with environmental progress in different areas such as **renewable** and clean energy programs. Space exploration is a way that Elon can help humans one day live on another planet, and renewable and clean energy is

---

renewable /ri-ˈnü-ə-bəl/ adjective: capable of being renewed or replaced <example: renewable resources>

one way he can help humans live better on Earth!

Although he doesn't have much free time, Elon Musk still has some hobbies. He occasionally binge watches TV shows. He tried making his own music for a short period of time and even released a song called "Don't Doubt Your Vibe" in 2020.

Perhaps Elon's favorite hobby is reading. Elon has read a lot throughout his life, and especially during his childhood, but he still makes time for it. He likes to read a range of types of books from science fiction and fantasy to biographies. He thinks that reading a book is one of the best ways to learn!

ADAM KENT

CHAPTER 5
FUN FACTS

1. There are many non-profit organizations operating in the United States. In fact, there are just under 2 million non-profits registered as of 2020.

2. Charitable organizations rely on donations from people. Most of the money, about 70%, that charities receive come from individuals.

3. December is the month of the year when the most donations are made.

ADAM KENT

CHAPTER 6
A PERSONAL LIFE

As of 2022, Elon Musk has been married twice. He also has several children. He has more children than the average family!

In 2000, Elon married his first wife who is named Justine Wilson. Elon met Justine in college. During their marriage, they had six children. Tragically, their first child, Nevada, passed away at just ten weeks old. As you can imagine it was a very sad time for both Justine and Elon.

Justine and Elon went on to have more children. Their next children were twins, named Griffin and Xavier. After that they had **triplets** named Kai, Saxon and Damian. You might be surprised by the fact that they had twins and triplets. This fact is thanks to science! Elon Musk and his wife Justine had the help of their doctors and a special medical **procedure** that makes it possible to have twins and triplets by choice and not chance. Altogether, they

---

procedure /prə-'sē-jər/ noun: a series of steps followed in a particular order to accomplish something *<example: a medical procedure>*

triplet /'tri-plət/ noun: a set or group of three *<example: She had triplets.>*

have five living children.

Sadly, Elon Musk and Justine Wilson did not stay married. Elon was very busy with work, and this caused some problems in their marriage. They decided to divorce. After Elon Musk and Justine Wilson divorced, Elon met a girl named Talulah Riley. She was an English actress. She was from England. The two fell in love quickly and got also married quickly in 2010. Unfortunately, after an up and down relationship, the marriage also did not last, and the couple divorced in 2016.

Elon Musk has also famously dated an American actress named Amber Heard in 2016, after she was divorced from the American actor Johnny Depp, who starred in many movies including the popular "Pirates of the Caribbean." The relationship did not last long though.

After dating Amber Heard, Elon Musk met and started dating the lady who would become the mother to his other children. She is a musician called Grimes, who is from Canada. Grimes's real name is Claire Boucher.

One interesting fact is that shortly after beginning to date Grimes, Elon encouraged her to change her name to "c," which is the math symbol for speed of light. Guess what? She did! It is unclear how often she uses that name, though. People still know her mainly as Grimes and Claire.

Elon and Grimes have had two children together in the time since they started dating. Grimes gave birth to a boy named "X Æ A-12" on May 4, 2020. Yes, the boy's name is X Æ A-12. His first name is "X."

Would you like to know how to pronounce that? According to Elon, the pronunciation is: "X like the letter X, then Ash, then A and 12." Grimes has actually explained the pronunciation differently. She once explained that the pronunciation is: "X like the letter, then A, then I, then A, then 12."

Shortly after naming their boy that, it was reported that the State of California wouldn't accept a name with a number. The couple said they were changing their son's name to "X Æ A-XII." XII is the

Roman numeral symbol for the number 12.

You might be wondering why they named their child that? Both Grimes and Elon are interesting and unique people. They have explained that each part of the name has special significance to them:

X = the unknown variable (as in equations)
Æ= the fairy version of AI, which stands for artificial intelligence

In December of 2021, Elon Musk and Grimes had a second child, a girl. They named her Exa Dark Sideræl Musk. They gave her the nickname of "Y." Elon and Grimes have chosen two unique names for their children! While they never married, they both remain committed to raising their two children together and also plan to remain good friends.

In 2022, it became known that Elon Musk also had twins with someone who worked for him at his company Neuralink. Her name is Shivon Zilis. They had the twins secretly, so not much is known about the choice or the relationship.

Elon Musk has publicly said that he thinks it is best for the future that people have more children. Over the years, families have had fewer children. Elon thinks that families should have more to keep up with the need for workers to help with technology and to care for a big older population.

Not everyone agrees with this belief! One thing is for sure, Elon is not just talking the talk. He is walking the walk by having much more children than the average family now.

CHAPTER 6
FUN FACTS

1. The chance of a mother having twins naturally, without the help of science, is about 1 in 250.

2. The chance of having triplets naturally, without the help of science, is about 1 in 10,000.

3. Elon Musk has had two sets of twins! The first was with his first wife, Justine. The second was with someone who worked at Neuralink, one of his companies, Shivon Zilis.

4. Elon Musk's children with the musician Grimes are nicknamed "X" and "Y."

CHAPTER 7

A LASTING LEGACY

Elon Musk's incredible legacy is like a rocket of inspiration that will keep soaring through time. He used his big imagination to change the world in amazing ways. With companies like Tesla and SpaceX, he showed us that dreams can become reality.

Elon's electric cars zoom silently, helping to keep our planet clean and green. His rockets teach us that there's no limit to where our dreams can take us. He even made a tunnel to beat traffic—how cool is that?

But Elon Musk's legacy is not just about machines. It's also about being brave and never giving up. He faced challenges but kept on trying, showing us that even failure can be a steppingstone to success. So, let Elon Musk's story be a spark that lights up your own dreams. Just like Musk, with your imagination and determination, you can create a better future for yourself and perhaps the world.

INSPIRATIONAL QUOTES

Quotes are like magical words that can lift your spirits and make you feel like you can conquer the world! They are short and powerful sentences that carry big messages. Quotes come from inspiring people who have experienced many things in life. They teach us valuable lessons, remind us to be brave, and encourage us to follow our dreams.

So, whenever you need some inspiration or a little boost of confidence, just read a quote, and you'll feel like you can achieve anything! Here are a few quotes from Elon Musk to inspire you on your way!

" People should pursue what they are passionate about. That will give them more pleasure than pretty much anything else."

" If you get up in the morning and think the future is going to be better, it is a bright day. Otherwise, it's not."

" Rockets are cool. There's no getting around that."

" Life is too short for long term grudges."

" For my part, I will never give up. I mean never.

" Some people don't like change, but you need to embrace change if the alternative is disaster.

" Failure is an option here. If things are not failing, you are not innovating enough."

" When something is important enough, you do it even if the odds are not in your favor."

" To our knowledge, life exists on only one planet, Earth. If something bad happens, it's gone. I think we should establish life on another planet--Mars in particular--but we're not making very good progress. SpaceX is intended to make that happen.

" I think that's the single best piece of advice: constantly think about how you could be doing things better and questioning yourself."

" The first step is to establish that something is possible; then probability will occur."

" I would like to die on Mars. Just not on impact."

" Persistence is very important. You should not give up unless you are forced to give up."

" Great companies are built on great products."

" Some people don't like change, but you need to embrace change if the alternative is disaster."

" My biggest mistake is probably weighing too much on someone's talent and not someone's personality. I think it matters whether someone has a good heart."

" It's very important to like the people you work with; otherwise, life and your job is gonna be quite miserable."

" My motivation for all my companies has been to be involved in something that I thought would have a significant impact on the world."

" I think the best way to predict the future is to invent it."

" People should pursue what they're passionate about. That will make them happier than pretty much anything else."

BOOK
DISCUSSION

How do you think that Elon's upbringing contributed to his success?

_____
_____
_____
_____
_____
_____

What other factors do you think contributed to Elon's success?

_____
_____
_____
_____
_____
_____

When Elon Musk was bullied as a kid, what do you think about him choosing to learn karate?

_____
_____
_____
_____
_____
_____

What do you think of Elon wanting to create commercial space exploration?

_____
_____
_____
_____
_____
_____

What do you think of the names of Elon Musk's children?

_____
_____
_____
_____
_____
_____

ADAM KENT

GLOSSARY

affordable /ə-ˈfȯr-də-bəl/ adjective: reasonably priced <example: an affordable car>

avid /ˈa-vəd/ adjective: having great enthusiasm or excitement for something *<example: an avid football fan>*

citizen /ˈsi-tə-zən/ noun 1: a person who lives in a certain place 2: a person who legally belongs to a certain place and has the rights and protections of that place *<example: a citizen of Canada>*

client /ˈklī-ənt/ noun: a person who uses the service of another *<example: a lawyer's clients>*

commercial /kə-'mər-shəl/ noun: an advertisement on internet, radio or television *<example: a television commercial>* adjective: related to the buying and selling of goods and services *<example: a commercial real estate property>*

controversial /ˌkän-trə-'vər-shəl/ adjective: related to or causing disagreement or argument <example: a controversial choice>

dietician /dī-ə-'ti-shən/ noun: a specialist that uses the science of nutrition to plan diets or food that people eat *<example: A dietician helped me lose weight.>*

diverse /dī-'vərs/ adjective 1: different or unlike *<example: diverse interests>* 2: made up of things or people that are different *<example: diverse groups of people>*

economics /ˌe-kə-'nä-miks/ noun: the study of how wealth is created by the making and selling of goods and services *<example: He studied economics in school.>*

engineer /ˌen-jə-'nir/ noun: a person who designs and builds useful machines (such as computers) or structures (such as buildings or roads) *<example: an electrical engineer>* verb: to plan, build or manage as a professional engineer *<example: He engineered*

a plan to improve the safety of the railroad track.>

entrepreneur /ˌän-trə-p(r)ə-'nər/ noun: a person who tries to make money by starting a business and managing it, as a company or alone, and all the risks that go with it *<example: She wanted to become an entrepreneur and start her own real estate business.>*

lavish /'la-vish/ adjective 1: a large amount *<example: a lavish display flowers>* 2: given in large amounts *<example: he received lavish praise>* verb: to give in large amounts *<example: he lavished her with praise>*

mannequin /'ma-ni-kən/ noun: a form that represents a human figure used for various purposes but especially for hanging clothes *<example: She dressed the mannequin with her clothing designs.>*

noteworthy /'nōt-,wər-t͟hē/ adjective: worthy of attracting attention *<example: a noteworthy event>*

physics /'fi-ziks/ noun: a science that deals with matter and energy and the interactions of both *<example: the study of physics>*

procedure /prə-'sē-jər/ noun: a series of steps followed in a particular order to accomplish something *<example: a medical procedure>*

renewable /ri-'nü-ə-bəl/ adjective: capable of being renewed or replaced *<example: renewable resources>*

satellite /'sa-tə-ˌlīt/ noun: something that orbits or exists near to another of larger size *<example: a satellite in space>*

transition /tran(t)-'si-shən/ noun: a change or shift from one to another state, subject or place *<example: transition of power>*

tribulation /ˌtri-byə-'lā-shən/ noun: a hard or distressing experience *<example: the*

tribulations of a difficult relationship>

triplet /'tri-plət/ noun: a set or group of three *<example: She had triplets.>*

venture /'ven(t)-shər / noun 1: an act that involves risk *<example: business venture>* verb 1: to guess at the risk of being wrong or criticised *<example: venture a guess>* 2: to go even though there is risk *<example: venture into the forest>*

ADAM KENT

REFERENCES

Dolan, Kerry A. "How To Raise a Billionaire: An Interview with Elon Musk's Father, Errol Musk". Forbes.

Elon Musk. (2018, April 4). Retrieved from https://www.biography.com/business-figure/elon-musk

"Frequently Asked Questions". hq.nasa.gov. May 4, 2016.

Gordon, Devin (March 10, 2022). "Infamy Is Kind of Fun": Grimes on Music, Mars, and—Surprise! —Her Secret New Baby with Elon Musk". Vanity Fair. Condé Nast.

Heathman, Amelia. "Elon Musk's boring machine has already built a 'test trench' in LA". Wired UK.

Hull, Dana; May, Patrick (April 10, 2014). "2014: Rocket Man: The otherworldly ambitions of Elon Musk". The Mercury News. September 6, 2016.

May, Dana Hull and Patrick. "Exploring the otherworldly ambitions of Elon Musk". The Buffalo News.

"Military Service Age and Obligation". World Factbook. March 8, 2019.

"Multiple Pregnancy and Birth: Twins, Triplets, and High Order Multiples (booklet)". *www.reproductivefacts.org*.

Regalado, Antonio (August 30, 2020). "Elon Musk's Neuralink is neuroscience theater". MIT Technology Review. December 13, 2020.

Smith, Adam (June 28, 2021). "50 years of Elon Musk's huge wealth, from emeralds to SpaceX and Tesla". The Independent. November 25, 2021.

Usborne, Simon (February 21, 2018). "Meet the Musks: who's who in

Elon's extended family?". The Guardian.

Williams, David (2018). "Mars Fact Sheet". NASA Goddard Space Flight Center. March 17, 2020.

LETTER FROM THE AUTHOR

Dear Readers,

I hope you enjoyed this book and learned some take away that may help you as you continue to grow and make choices in life. Reading biographies of famous people can help us learn about ourselves and what decisions help and hurt people as they follow their dreams. If you enjoyed learning about this icon, you can read about more in our kids biographies series!

Happy learning and may your dreams come true!

All the best,

Adam Kent

ADAM KENT

COLLECT THE WHOLE
GET SMART BOOK SERIES

Here are just a few:

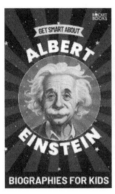  

Join our book club for free book offers. For more info email:

info@rocketkidsbookclub.com

Made in the USA
Monee, IL
18 November 2024

70434783R00061